THE ARCHITECTURE AND INFRASTRUCTURE OF BRITAIN'S RAILWAYS

West Midlands, Wales and the West

Patrick Bennett

AMBERLEY

First published 2019

Amberley Publishing
The Hill, Stroud
Gloucestershire, GL5 4EP

www.amberley-books.com

Copyright © Patrick Bennett, 2019

The right of Patrick Bennett to be identified as
the Author of this work has been asserted in
accordance with the Copyrights, Designs and
Patents Act 1988.

ISBN 978 1 4456 8153 5 (print)
ISBN 978 1 4456 8154 2 (ebook)

British Library Cataloguing in Publication Data.
A catalogue record for this book is available from
the British Library.

Origination by Amberley Publishing.
Printed in the UK.

Contents

Introduction

In the area covered by this book two railway companies predominate – the Great Western and the London & North Western; the former is mostly in the West of England, the South Midlands and South Wales, with the latter in North and Mid-Wales, and the West and North Midlands. The GWR was the inheritor of some of the most elegant mid-nineteenth-century buildings, mostly as a result of the influence of Isambard Kingdom Brunel. The London & North Western benefitted from the early work of Francis Thompson, particularly in North Wales. The North Staffordshire Railway, also featured here, produced some remarkably elegant buildings and seemed to take particular care in all its structures. A number of other companies are represented in these pages, including the Midland, Barry, Cambrian, Wirral, Mersey, London & South Western, Birkenhead Joint and the Cheshire Lines Committee.

The traditional signal box and its associated semaphore signalling is probably the most iconic symbol of the old railway. Sadly the 'box' is an endangered species, and in the coming years signalling for the whole network will be controlled from just fourteen centres. Many of the signal boxes shown here have been abolished, and more will follow shortly. Recognising the importance of this part of railway heritage, the Signalling Study Group set out to record and classify all known types of signal box. It is the SSG system of classification which has been used in this volume.

Another symbol of the old railway is the goods shed. Nowadays little regarded, goods sheds and depots were once the backbone of the railway industry, since for many companies income from freight traffic far exceeded that from passengers. Only in recent years has this significance been recognised, and a number of goods sheds and related facilities now have protected status. The buildings themselves come in all shapes and sizes, from some the size of a garden shed to the massive city centre depots. This diversity is reflected in these pages. Also shown are collieries, coal concentration depots, transhipment sheds and other facilities connected with the transport of freight.

The railways of Britain were a complex, integrated system and there are many aspects of the railway other than those mentioned above. Not least of these is the permanent way, some of the most spectacular parts of which were the bridges and viaducts. Also shown here are structures relating to water supplies, office and staff accommodation, hotels and carriage sheds.

Historic England and Coflein in Wales classify important buildings in the following manner:

Grade I – buildings of exceptional interest.
Grade II* – particularly important buildings of more than special interest.
Grade II – buildings of special interest.

These gradings are noted in the text.

The author and publisher would like to thank the following people for permission to use copyright material in this book: Ben Brooksbank for the photograph of Aberystwyth station, and Richard Rogerson for the photograph of Cardiff station.

Patrick Bennett
Millay, France
November 2018

Stations

Great Western Railway

The first station at Wrexham General was built by the Shrewsbury & Chester Railway in 1848. The second, constructed by the GWR in 1912, utilised stone from the first. It is in a French turn-of-the-century style built of coursed rubble with ashlar mullions, lintels and other dressings. The two pavilions either side of the entry have elaborate cast-iron crestings. There are later brick additions at either end of the main building.

Gobowen station was designed by Thomas Penson and built for the S&C in 1848. It is in a Tuscan style complete with a 'campanile', built of stucco-covered brick. The branch to Oswestry, the former headquarters of the Cambrian Railway, still exists and is the home of Cambrian Heritage Railways. Grade II listed.

Another building in a similar Italianate style is Albrighton, built by the Shrewsbury & Birmingham Railway in 1849. It is of brick with painted ashlar dressings and it has an interesting quadruple chimney. Grade II listed.

The line from Kingswinford Junction to Oxley Junction was started in 1858 but it was to be another sixty-seven years before it was completed throughout. Wombourne, the principal station on the line, was opened in 1925 and closed to passengers just seven years later. It remained open for freight until 1965 when the majority of the line was closed. It is a pleasant building in red brick with a plinth in Staffordshire blue bricks. It remains as a tearoom on the South Staffordshire Walk.

The Newport, Abergavenny & Hereford Railway opened to goods in July 1852 and to passengers in January 1854. The NA&H did not actually reach Newport but met the Monmouthshire Railway & Canal Company's line at Pontypool, which it used to reach Newport. Of the original nine stations between Hereford and Pontypool, only Abergavenny remains open. Pontrilas closed in 1958. The surviving building is in coursed rubble with ashlar dressings and a slate roof. Also with a slate roof is the canopy, which has a sawtooth canopy.

The first station at Aberystwyth was opened in 1864 and subsequently altered and enlarged. In 1924–5 a new station building designed by Harris & Sheppard was constructed by the GWR. It is a classical two-storey ashlar building. The central thirteen-bay section is flanked by two three-bay pavilions. At the east end is a somewhat truncated four-sided clock tower which has pedimented and pilastered frames to each face. Grade II listed. (Photo: Ben Brooksbank)

The present building at Cardiff Central dates only from 1932 to 1934. Designed by the GWR architect's department under the Unemployment Relief Scheme it is another ashlar building in Portland stone. The five-bay central section is flanked by two three-bay pavilions with pediments on two sides. 'Great Western Railway' is emblazoned across the frontage, above which sits a curiously old-fashioned-looking clock tower. (Photo: Richard Rodgerson)

The GWR completed the line from Didcot to Oxford in 1844 and the delightful little station at Culham dates from that broad-gauge period. It is the last surviving example of a Brunel-designed Tudor-style station on the GWR. It is built of brick with ashlar dressings. A feature seen elsewhere in Brunel-designed stations is the flat all-round canopy, supported on decorative brackets. The station was originally known as Abingdon Road. Grade II* listed.

Appleford, just south of Culham, also opened in 1844 but was closed again just a few years later. It was reopened in 1933 as Appleford Halt, and remains open today as simply Appleford. Until at least the 1990s it retained its wooden platforms and 'pagoda' shelters, as seen here. Sadly both the wooden platforms and pagodas have now gone, leaving Denham Golf Club as the only station on the network still retaining this once common kind of shelter.

There were once two stations at Aynho: Aynho Park on the Chiltern Line, and Aynho for Deddington on the Oxford and Rugby line, the station seen here. It has some stylistic similarities to Culham, principally the all-round canopy with valancing supported on decorative brackets. It is built of coursed rubble with ashlar dressings. It is now a private house.

In 1845 the Oxford, Worcester & Wolverhampton Railway was authorised to build a railway from Oxford to Wolverhampton. It earned its sobriquet (The Old Worse and Worse), among other reasons, for the length of time it took to complete the line, just 90 miles long. It finally opened throughout on 1 December 1853. The engineer for the line was I. K. Brunel, and Charlbury was a station built to his design. Brunel often built in wood, as here, but very few such buildings have survived. The hipped roof also forms the canopy, which is supported on carved wooden brackets. The wooden benches and the running-in board, as well as the building itself, are all listed Grade II.

The original 1854 building at Wolverhampton built for the OWW by John Fowler was subsequently altered and enlarged. Built of blue brick with ashlar dressings, the original building in an Italianate style consisted of a central two-storey, five-bay block flanked by a seven-bay wing to either side, terminating in a three-bay pavilion. Later a second storey was added to the left-hand wing. Following the ending of passenger services in 1972, the station became a parcels depot, which had recently ceased operations when this photograph was taken. Latterly the platforms and ancillary buildings have been demolished, being replaced by a large block of flats. The main station building is now an event venue. Grade II listed.

The present station at Kemble dates only from 1872. Although the Swindon to Gloucester line opened in 1845 there had previously been only a platform here for passengers to change for the Cirencester branch. The station is in a pleasant Tudor style, built of Cotswold stone. Notable features are the coped gables with kneelers on the north side and the splayed slit openings. There is also a substantial canopy. Kemble was also the junction for Tetbury. This branch closed in 1964 along with the branch to Cirencester. Grade II listed.

Bradford-on-Avon station was completed in 1848, nine years before it ever saw a train. The Wilts, Somerset & Weymouth Railway, whose project this was, ran into financial trouble and was unable to complete its line. Despite being taken over by the GWR in 1850, it was to be another seven years before Bradford received its rails and trains started running. The buildings are Brunel-inspired, built of Bath stone in a Tudor style. The canopy on the Trowbridge platform (on the right in this view) is original; the other is a later GWR replacement. Grade II listed.

Frome didn't have to wait for quite so long. In October 1850 a branch to Frome was completed, and another from Frome to Radstock started, although that line was not completed until 1854. Frome station, seen here in 1990, is the last surviving wooden GWR station with an overall roof. Grade II listed.

Warminster was also intended to be a station on the WS&W but was actually built by the GWR in 1851, which by then had absorbed the WS&W. It remained a terminus for the next five years until the line was extended to Salisbury in 1856. It is a plain, lapped-boarded building, redeemed to some extent by the pierced, sawtooth valancing. Like Frome it originally had an overall roof but this has not survived.

The word sublime does not seem too strong to describe this superb Brunellian station built by the Bristol & Exeter Railway. Shown here is the booking hall with its veranda supported on cast-iron brackets. It has a high parapet with a moulded coping and plinth and a small pediment. The sash windows have been retained, as has much of the interior furniture. The whole station is well presented and is worth inspection. Dating from the opening of the line in 1841, these buildings are listed Grade II*.

The station buildings at Taunton have been modified a number of times but the two-storey block and single-storey wing are part of the original station of 1842. The main block is in white brick and has a concealed roof behind a parapet and cornice. The sash windows show similarities with those at Bridgwater. The canopies on cast-iron brackets are a later GWR addition. It looks as though a start was made on cleaning the brickwork but the job was never completed. Grade II listed.

The first station at Exeter St David's was designed by Brunel but a major rebuilding took place in 1864 to the designs of Francis Fox and Henry Lloyd. The main building is a two-storey block built of random rubble with ashlar dressings. The central three bays are surmounted by a balustrade. In front of the two-storey block is a single-storey block in the same style, to the centre of which an additional storey in ashlar was added in 1911.

Dawlish station was opened by the South Devon Railway in 1846. The present building dates from 1875 and presents entirely different aspects on the landward and seaward sides. The former is an Italianate building in rusticated stucco (see inset), while the latter consists of a granite-faced building on a battered stone base. Curiously, the return is the sole feature on the seaward side in stucco. Notice the walkway leading to the board crossing supported on cast-iron columns. Grade II listed.

In 1927 a new station building was opened at Newton Abbot to the design of the Chief Architect of the GWR, Percy Culverhouse. This is a nicely symmetrical building constructed in red brick with ashlar dressings in 'Wrennaissance' style. It is nine bays wide, the centre three bays being three storeys high with a dentilled pediment. The two wings have a Mansard roof above a dentilled cornice.

Despite being authorised in 1846, the Cornwall Railway did not open until 4 May 1859, and then only between Plymouth and Truro. The second station in Cornwall is St Germans. The buildings have no great architectural merit but at least original buildings have been retained on both platforms. With rather nice stone chimney stacks but otherwise looking extremely tatty in this 1990 view, this is the Up platform.

Menheniot is the next station along the line. This building is all there is for the comfort of passengers but at least it is original, dating from the opening of the line. In 1990 it was clearly in need of a repaint, which thankfully it has since received. Notice the GWR milepost, which indicates 261¾ miles from Paddington.

Liskeard has in effect two stations. The main building sits high above the platforms. It is built in rendered stone and has a nice canopy supported on cast-iron spandrels. The second building, which is at a right angle to the main line, is for the Looe branch. The Caradon Railway had worked the trains to Looe since 1860, but it was only in 1901 that the line reached Liskeard station, at which time the second station was opened, this time in wood.

The Newquay branch largely owed its existence to the Cornwall Minerals Railway, which was authorised in 1873, although there had been railways in the area for some years, which had been absorbed by the CMR. From 1877 the CMR was leased to the GWR, by which it was purchased in 1901. There were five stations on the line, all of which survive. Roche is a request stop with a very sparse service. A more substantial wooden building once existed on the opposite platform when Roche was a passing place but this has long since disappeared.

Bugle, next station along the line, clearly warranted a larger shelter, as seen here, but even this has now gone, replaced by the most minimal of 'bus shelters'. Bugle was the junction for the Carbis branch, which closed in 1989.

Truro was the meeting place of the broad gauge Cornwall Railway and the standard gauge West Cornwall Railway, although the latter later laid a third rail to enable broad gauge trains to reach Penzance. The station was rebuilt in 1897 and the fin de siècle influence is clear in the two French-style pavilions with their crested roofs. Otherwise it is a single-storey building in red brick with contrasting blue brick for the plinth and window surrounds. The slate roof has a very nice roof light.

The original station at Penzance was another Brunel-designed edifice constructed of wood and had an overall roof. The present station dates from 1879 and was designed by William Owen. It is built of stone and has an unusual crescent-trussed iron and glass roof. The glass alone weighs 50 tons. The three platforms seen here were joined by a fourth alongside the train shed in 1937.

London & North Western Railway

The Chester & Holyhead Railway was opened from Chester to Bangor on 1 May 1848. The architect for the stations was Francis Thompson. Flint station consists of a central three-bay section flanked by two single-bay pavilions. Construction is of brick with nice ashlar embellishments to the sash windows on the first floor. It is unfortunate that one of the ground-floor pavilions has been somewhat unsympathetically altered. It has been impossible to discover to what the coat of arms relates.

In 1897 the LNWR, successor to the CHR, quadrupled the tracks along a large part of the Chester–Holyhead line. This entailed building a new station at Prestatyn some distance away from the original, which is shown here. This is a Francis Thompson-designed building of 1848, consisting of a two-storey central section with single-storey projecting wings. Next to the station stands the contemporaneous goods shed built of snecked rubble.

Holywell Junction, as its name implies, was the junction for the 1¾-mile branch to Holywell. The station is considered to be the best of Thompson's design for the CHR. It is a two-storey square building in dark brick with a concealed roof. The mouldings above the ground floor arched windows have rose motifs, which are repeated in the frieze below the cornice. Holywell station closed in 1954 and Holywell Junction in 1966. Grade II listed.

Llong was a station on the Mold Railway line that ran from Saltney to Mold, which opened in 1849. In 1869 the line was extended to Denbigh. The station building, seen here in 1990 still in original condition, is strikingly similar to the old station at Prestatyn; unsurprisingly so since Llong was also the work of Thompson. The station closed in 1962, although the line remained open for freight until 1983.

Malpas was one of the three stations on the LNW line which ran from Tattenhall Junction to Whitchurch. It opened in 1872, closing to passenger traffic in 1959 and to freight in 1963. The building has hardly changed since closure though it has lost its platform canopy, the supports for which are still present. It is built of roughhewn, coursed, sandstone rubble with ashlar door and window dressings, also in sandstone. The decorative bargeboards are original.

The railway to Knighton opened in 1861. The station is in a curious mixture of styles – Gothic combined with rugged cottage orné. The buildings are of coursed rock-faced limestone rubble with ashlar dressings. The main building shown here is the stationmaster's house. Notice the decorative fish scale roof tiles, and not forgetting the two-tone Ford Consul! Grade II listed.

Goostrey, a station on the Manchester–Crewe main line, is included here as an example of the LNW's prefabricated wooden station buildings. The modules were manufactured at Crewe Works, before being sent out by train and assembled on site. By using different numbers of the standard modules it was possible to construct stations of varying sizes. Goostrey station was a late arrival on the scene, opening in 1891.

Buxton once had two identical stations, those of the LNWR and MR, both designed by Joseph Paxton, of Crystal Palace fame. The Midland station has been demolished and the LNW building has lost its overall roof, leaving just this end screen. Grade II listed.

Curzon Street was the northern terminus of the London & Birmingham Railway, which opened in 1838. It was designed in a Greek Revival style by Philip Hammond. It is a square three-storey building fronted by a giant order of four Ionic columns. Above this is an entablature with stepped architrave, blank frieze and dentilled cornice, which continues round the building. Demolition was proposed in the 1970s but thankfully the building survived and is listed Grade I.

After two failed attempts the LNW opened a line from Aston to Sutton Coldfield in 1862. There were two intermediate stations, including Chester Road shown here. These modest prefabricated wooden buildings have been swept away and replaced by an even more modest arrangement of ultra-modern canopies but with no other buildings.

It was always intended to extend the Sutton Coldfield branch northwards to Lichfield, and this was finally achieved in 1884, when Shenstone station was opened. It is a nice example of Domestic Revival architecture. Features of note are the use of windows in groups, the decorated ridges terminating in finials, the huge decorative bargeboards and the pointed arches over the windows.

Woburn Sands is included here as an example of cottage orné style, popular in the mid-nineteenth century. Characteristic features are the half-timbering, fretted bargeboards and a projecting gable. There are several other stations on the Bedford–Bletchley line in a similar style. In this 1989 photograph a Class 108 DMU arrives with a service for Bedford. Since that time the line has been resignalled and the signal box abolished. Grade II listed.

Designed by J. W. Livock and opened for the Trent Valley Railway in 1847, Atherstone station is an unspoilt gem. In Tudor style and built of brick with limestone dressings, it has many notable features. Among these are the coped gable parapets with octagonal finials at the apex and on the kneelers; bands of fish scale tiles; octagonal and square chimney stacks; and the windows with stone mullions and transoms. It is now used as offices. Grade II listed.

North Staffordshire Railway

The station at Rushton is situated on the former Churnet Valley line. Opened in 1844, it closed to passengers in 1960 and to freight in 1964. It is constructed of coursed and dressed limestone rubble. It has coped gable parapets with kneelers and bands of fish scale tiles in the roof. It has a collection of round, square and diamond-shaped chimney stacks. Grade II listed.

Stoke-on-Trent station dates from 1847 to a design by H. A. Hunt. It is a two-storey brick and stone building in a 'Jacobethan' style. The central section consists of three Dutch gables with diapering in blue brick, below which is an advanced colonnade of Doric columns. Above this is a frieze and a fretwork parapet. Grade II* listed.

By contrast is Stockton Brook, a simple single-storey lapped-boarded building with a slate roof. The Stoke to Leek line opened in 1867 but the station here did not open until 1896, and closed in 1956. The line remained in use for freight until 1988. Today the track is owned by the Moorland & City Railway, in effect an offshoot of the Churnet Valley Railway.

Alsager station was opened in 1848. The station house seen here is constructed of red brick in Flemish bond with painted stone dressings and diapering in blue Staffordshire bricks. Decorative elements of the roof are alternate layers of different tiles, ridge tiles and bargeboards.

In a very similar style to Stoke, and unsurprisingly by the same architect, is Stone station. Once again we see Dutch gables, red brick with blue diapering and sandstone ashlar dressings. The centre bay has on the ground floor a three-arch loggia in stone. The flanking gables each have a cartouche but no detail is visible. Grade II listed.

Cheshire Lines Committee

The line between Northwich and Helsby was opened in 1870 by the West Cheshire Railway, later part of the CLC, itself owned by three railway companies, the MR, GNR and the MSL. Greenbank was originally Hartford & Greenbank, renamed Greenbank by BR in 1973. This 1989 view is of a well-proportioned combination of station and passenger facilities. A sad sign of the times is that all the ground floor doorways and windows have now either been bricked up or have grilles.

In contrast to Greenbank, Mouldsworth, further west, which was the junction of lines to Helsby and Chester, is constructed of rock-faced, coursed rubble with ashlar dressings. Happily Mouldsworth has not shared the same fate as Greenbank and retains all its original features. It is largely occupied as a private house.

The Midland, Cambrian, Wirral, Barry, and Mersey Railways

The MR opened the Ashchurch to Barnt Green line in 1864. The station at Evesham, which was adjacent to that of the GWR, was designed by George Hunt. A single-storey building of brick with two gables with triple round-arch windows, the remainder with segmental arches, the station closed to passengers in 1967 and freight in 1984.

Meols was one of the original stations of the Hoylake Railway, opening in 1866. The HR became part of the Wirral Railway in 1883 and part of the LMS at Grouping. The line was electrified in 1938 and at the same time the stations were rebuilt in art deco style. Meols is another station which has had most of it openings blocked up.

Ellesmere station was opened by the Oswestry, Ellesmere & Whitchurch Railway in 1863. For a year it was the terminus of the line from Whitchurch. Following merger with other companies to form the Cambrian Railways, the line was extended to Oswestry. Ellesmere became a junction in 1895 with the opening of the Great Central line from Wrexham Central. This line closed in 1962, with the Whitchurch–Oswestry line following in 1965. The building is constructed of brick in Flemish bond with two projecting gables on the south side. The ground floor windows have sandstone lintels and sills while those on the first floor have segmental keyed arches. Grade II listed.

The Barry Railway was formed by Rhondda mine owners in 1889 to give an independent outlet for the export of their coal. The BR was principally a mineral railway but in 1896 a branch to the seaside destination of Barry Island was opened. An initial 3-foot 6-inch gauge tramway was quickly replaced by a standard gauge line. The station building consists of a single storey with two projecting gables. Extensive use is made of stone for window dressings, string courses, quoins and copings. It has a Welsh slate roof with decorative ridge tiles. Since this picture was taken in 1992 a number of sympathetic additions have been made.

The Mersey Railway opened its line from Liverpool James Street to Green Lane in 1886. The two intermediate stations were Birkenhead Hamilton Square and Birkenhead Central. Various extensions eventually gave the railway a total length of 4 miles 46 chains. It is perhaps remarkable that such a tiny enterprise should remain independent right up to Nationalisation. Central was a rather splendid station for such a small railway. At the street level it was a single-storey building, and at platform level three storeys. There is a rather nice frontage at street level with a parapet decorated with ball finials. The platforms have nice canopies supported on a double row of cast-iron columns.

Joint Railways

The Birkenhead Railway was formed in 1859 and taken over in 1860 by the GWR and LNWR to become the Birkenhead Joint. Its lines formed a triangle from Birkenhead and West Kirby to Chester and Warrington. It remained a joint railway until Nationalisation. Frodsham station opened in 1850. 'Jacobethan' in style, it has a five-bay central section with a projecting gable and single-storey wings. It is built of brick with ashlar quoins, copings, and door and window dressings. The station has now been cleaned and refurbished to a very high standard and is in private hands. Grade II listed.

Hereford station, originally Hereford Barrs Court, was jointly owned by the GWR and LNWR. The Midland Railway had access rights. Completed in 1854 to the design of R. E. Johnston, it is a nice example of Mid-Victorian Gothic. Of note are the lancet windows in rusticated stone panels, the groups of chimneys and the octagonal finials. Grade II listed.

The construction of the line from St Budeaux Victoria Road to Gunnislake included no less than four different railway companies. They were the LSWR, the Plymouth, Devonport & South Western Junction, the Bere Alston & Calstock Light and the East Cornwall Mineral Railway. Following the closure of the route to Exeter via Tavistock, Bere Alston was no longer a junction but trains still have to reverse here to reach Gunnislake. The station building is constructed of snecked rubble with ashlar door and window dressings. The platform has retained its canopy.

The GW/GC Joint line between Northolt and Ashendon Junction opened in 1905. Denham Golf Club was opened in 1912 at the request of the adjacent golf club. It is now unique in being the last station on the network to retain the once common 'pagoda' shelters. The booking office at the foot of the path to the platforms was in the same style. Unfortunately this was vandalised beyond repair and has been replaced by a replica. On 25 May 1989 a Class 115 DMU enters the station with a Banbury–Marylebone service. Grade II listed.

London & South Western Railway

Whimple station was opened in 1860 when the LSW extended its line from Yeovil to Exeter. The station building was designed by Sir William Tite, who did much work for the LSW. It is in a more or less Tudor style with four centre window arches and decorative barge boards, but little else of note. Whimple was a station proposed for closure in the Beeching Report.

Another station proposed for closure was Topsham on the Exeter–Exmouth line. The whole line was proposed for closure. It is another station designed by Tite, again in a loosely Tudor style. The single-storey wing is of brick with ashlar dressings, while the remainder of the building is in painted brickwork. It has retained its four huge chimney stacks. Grade II listed.

The station buildings at Exeter Central date from 1933. They consist of a central rectangular block with two curved wings, thus forming a crescent. The main building is Georgian in style, constructed of brick with ashlar window dressings and plinth. Also of stone is the dentilled parapet, behind which sits a half-hipped roof, which formerly had a turret. Above the three entrance doors are rather nice lunettes.

Details

GWR benches through the ages: top left, at Barry, the Victorian version; top right, 1930s art deco at Truro; bottom left, also at Truro, the BR version; and bottom right, also seen at Truro, is this bench with its own individual shelter, almost certainly Victorian.

Many stations had benches with the station name. Here are two examples in different styles.

Some railway stations had quite extraordinary embellishment. This faience work is part of the decoration of the waiting room on the east platform at Worcester Shrub Hill. The tiles were by Maw & Co. Grade II* listed.

Another extraordinary station is Great Malvern. Each of the column capitals supporting the canopy is decorated with wrought iron foliage in a different style. This was the work of William Forsyth. Grade II listed.

Elaborate ironwork at Llandudno station. Notice in particular the LMS monogram.

This is the family crest of the 3rd Baron Mostyn, as it appears on the closed Mostyn station. The Welsh translates approximately as: 'Without God, Without Anything, God is Enough'.

On the platform at Mouldsworth is this survivor from another age. The luggage trolley is painted with 'CLC Mouldsworth', while the wheel hubs have the letters 'LMSR'. Notice the wheel chock.

Delivering the Goods

Large Goods Sheds and Depots

Although the GWR and MR shared the station at Worcester Shrub Hill, for goods traffic they each had their own facilities. Both goods sheds survive in commercial use. This is the MR depot: a brick building with a ridge and furrow roof with a two-storey office block at one end. Both the blind arches and window arches are picked out in white brick.

The goods shed at Hereford is also of red brick, with decoration amounting only to brick pilasters dividing the bays. Note that there are six cart docks, though unevenly spaced. There is a two-storey office block. On the opposite wall each bay has a multi-paned round-headed window. The building is now in use for bowling.

St Austell goods shed was built entirely of blue engineering bricks. It had a two-storey office block at one end and on the loading bay side it had a continuous canopy. It has not survived.

Rugeley Trent Valley goods shed consists of a gable-ended building with a single-storey office block at the south end. Built in brick, embellishment is minimal, consisting largely of panelled walls. Its unusual feature is a glass roofed *porte cochère* protecting the loading dock. The building is now in industrial use and happily the *porte cochère* roof has been reglazed.

Wednesfield Road Depot has an interesting history. Having lost its running powers into Wolverhampton High Level in June 1878, the MR decided to build a passenger station at Wednesfield Road. No sooner had the MR acquired its Act to build the station than Parliament decided to reassert the MR's right to run into Wolverhampton HL. So instead of building a passenger station the MR decided to build a goods depot. This was completed in 1881. It was constructed in blue and red brick in alternating bands, with stone for door and window dressings. The legend along the return reads: 'Midland Railway Goods and Grain Warehouse'. The depot was demolished shortly after this photograph was taken.

Medium-Sized Goods Sheds

Congleton goods shed, built in 1849 for the NSR, is unusual in two respects. Firstly, it is of the 'through' type for both rail and road vehicles, and secondly it has a hipped roof, unusual outside the NER area. The office seems unusually small for such a large shed.

Very few goods sheds were constructed of corrugated iron. This warehouse at Melksham must have been a hot place to work during the summer with sunlight streaming through the roof lights. When this photograph was taken in 1990 the building had recently been refurbished. Its present fate is unknown.

Less unusual was wood, as here at New Mills Central. Few timber goods sheds have survived, being subject to both rot and fire. New Mills Central is no exception. It was demolished to make way for housing. Notice the yard crane.

Where stone was plentiful this was often the material of choice. Chapel-en-le-Frith is in the Peak District, where there is an endless supply of millstone grit. The LNW and the MR both had stations at Chapel. The latter closed in 1967 but both the former station building and the goods shed survive in industrial use.

Further south in the Peak District limestone comes to the fore, as in this goods shed at Ashbourne. It is of the 'through' type and is built of squared and coursed limestone rubble. It retains the canopies covering the two cart docks. It is remarkably complete and unaltered yet for some reason it is not a listed building.

Another area replete with stone is Dartmoor, where we find Okehampon goods shed. Constructed of snecked granite rubble with cast-iron framed, round arch windows, it is of the through type with two cart docks permitting ingress and a loading bay with a canopy.

Stroud goods shed is a gem. Built to a Brunel standard design *c.* 1845, it is now the only survivor of the type. It is built of squared, coursed limestone rubble with ashlar dressings. On the south side it has three offset buttresses and two sets of four blocked lancets. It is of the 'through' type for both rail and road vehicles. The legend on the south wall reads: 'GWR STROUD STATION EXPRESS GOODS TRAIN SERVICES AND TRANSITS BEWEEN IMPORTANT TOWNS'. Grade II* listed.

The goods shed at Llanelli dates from 1875. It is built of snecked rubble with dressings of rock-faced stone. It has a timber-trussed roof. It is currently the focus of a local campaign to turn it into a community facility. Grade II listed.

Small Goods Sheds

Panelled walls, roof lights and louvred vents in the end walls are typical design elements of LNW goods sheds, as here at Wrenbury, on the Crewe–Shrewsbury line.

A rare survivor is this wooden NSR goods shed at Rushton. Lapped-boarded timber on a stone base, its minimalist design and construction was no impediment to doing its job for the local community.

Bromborough is on the Birkenhead Joint line to Chester. Surely one of the smallest goods sheds, it is built of brick in English bond. On the track side it has a narrow loading platform with a canopy, and on the road side a single cart dock.

Dating from 1903 is this small brick-built shed, also in English bond but relieved with quoins in contrasting blue brick. There is a single opening on each side. Hullavington is a closed station on the Bristol main line. Passenger services were withdrawn in 1961, while freight lingered on until 1965.

Bettisfield was a station on the former Cambrian line from Whitchurch to Oswestry. It lost its goods service in 1964 with passenger services following a year later. The goods shed is a rare survivor; only two other Cambrian goods sheds are known to have survived. A simple brick-built structure with panelled walls, it has been altered considerably to serve as apartments.

Waterhouses was the meeting place of the 2-foot 6-inch gauge Leek & Manifold Valley Light Railway and the NSR branch from Leek. The station was fully opened by 1905. Passenger services ceased in 1935 while goods continued until 1943. Of the buildings here, only the goods shed survives, used for cycle hire for the Manifold Way cycle route.

Weighbridges

Every goods yard had its weighbridge, always accompanied by a small hut containing the weighing equipment. This example is at Hullavington. Even with such an insignificant building some effort has been made with design, using contrasting brick for the quoins and window surround.

In 1989 Worcester Shrub Hill still retained its weighbridge and hut. The notice informs us that 'THE NORMAL CAPACITY FOR THIS MACHINE IS 20 TONS GROSS'.

Cattle, Oil, Limestone, Cement and Rubbish

These are the livestock pens at Oswestry. The carrying of livestock was an important business for the railway. The last cattle train ran in the early 1970s.

This was the situation at Thornton South Sidings, Stanlow, in 1993. Oil at that time clearly constituted a healthy flow for the railway. Since this photograph was taken all the sidings have disappeared. Rail transport of oil has been largely superseded by the use of pipelines.

One traffic that remains healthy is limestone. This is Great Rocks in the Peak District, where No. 37688 shunts a rake of the famous ICI bogie wagons.

Much limestone is used to make cement. Here we see the finished product being unloaded at the Blue Circle depot at Northenden. This train originated at Earle's Sidings. The locomotive is No. 37677.

One area where the railway has been successful is in the transport of household refuse. The Calvert landfill site is adjacent to the GC London Extension line. Trains arrive via the GW/GC Joint line through High Wycombe. In the foreground is the platform of the former Claydon station. If the East West Rail project ever comes to pass, trains will be extended through this point to reach the Oxford–Bletchley line at Claydon Junction.

Coal

This is Cynheidre Colliery, Carmarthenshire, seen shortly after closure in 1989. At the time of closure it had a workforce of 1,000.

Littleton Colliery is seen just a year before closure. Littleton regularly produced over a million tons of coal per year. The coal was destined for power stations. It was transported in HAA wagons, a few of which can be seen on the right.

While the HAA wagon was developed for MGR traffic, the HEA wagon (previously HBA) was introduced in the 1970s for domestic coal distribution. An example is seen here at Shrewsbury in 1991, when the coal depot was still active.

Formerly coal was delivered to every station, from where the merchants could deliver it to their customers. In the 1960s, in an effort to save costs, BR set up Coal Concentration Depots. This is Droitwich.

The CCDs had a very short life, as consumption of domestic coal was in rapid decline. In 1993 it formed just 7 per cent of the market for heating fuel. This is one of the sad remnants of Watford CCD, seen in 1992.

Transfer

This is part of the Wolverhampton Steel Terminal. It is perhaps not immediately apparent, but a branch of the Birmingham Canal terminates under the canopies, where goods were transferred between rail and canal. Needless to say this facility no longer exists. In the background is the Stour Valley line.

One of the problems of the broad gauge/standard gauge duality was the transfer of goods between systems. This is the transfer shed at Exeter St David's. The broad gauge wagons entered the left-hand arch. It is a brick building with an entablature and cornice in stone. The walls have alternate blind arches and round-arched windows. Grade II listed.

Signalling and Signs

Signal Boxes

Great Western Railway

Ystrad Mynach South signal box was built for the Rhymney Railway by McKenzie & Holland *c.* 1890. It is a Type 3. It was built on an embankment to give the signalman a clear view of the sweeping curve of the main line. As a result a special arrangement had to be constructed to bring the point rodding and signal wires down to rail level. Notice also the sighting boards behind the signals in the distance. The left-hand signal was for the Cwmbargoed branch. The box was abolished in 2013.

Tram Inn signal box, on the Hereford–Abergavenny line, is a much modified GWR Type 5. It dates from 1894 and as of 2018 remains open. Tram Inn station opened in 1853 and closed in 1958.

The signal box seen here was originally named Preesgweene. It was renamed Weston Rhyn in 1935. Dating from *c.* 1880, it is a McKenzie & Holland Type 3, fitted with a forty-seven-lever frame. The subsidiary signal is for the Down loop, since removed. The box itself was abolished in 1991. The frame and the upper part of the box went to the Llangollen Railway.

Yeovil Pen Mill is a GWR Type 7d signal box with an internal staircase. Somewhat unusually, the lower quadrant signals here have all recently been replaced by upper quadrants.

Langley Green is another GWR Type 7 signal box, with an unusual rear staircase. It was opened in 1904 and closed just ten months after this photograph was taken, in October 1989. Notice the white finials on the GWR signal posts. This was often to be found in areas taken over by the LMR. The subsidiary signal is for the Rood End sidings. The station was originally Langley Green & Rood End, and was the junction for the Oldbury branch. Oldbury station closed in 1916 but the line remained open for freight for many years after.

When it was abolished in 2012, Hartlebury Station box was one of the oldest working boxes on former GWR territory. It dates from 1876 and is a McKenzie & Holland Type 2. Very few of this type were built. In 1982 the frame was replaced by a panel.

McKenzie & Holland used the Type 3 design from 1875 to 1921. Baschurch box dates from 1880. It originally had a sixteen-lever frame but this was replaced by a twenty-five-lever frame and a gate wheel in 1911. The box was abolished in 1999. Grade II listed.

This was originally Truro East box, opened in 1899. Another example of a Type 7 box, it originally had a forty-five-lever frame, which was replaced in 1971 by a seventy-one-lever frame at the time that Truro West box was closed, when it was renamed simply 'Truro'. Note the sighting board. There is a Bachmann model based on Truro box.

The wooden version of the GWR Type 7 box is known as Type 27. This example at Liskeard is a Type 27c and has an internal staircase. It was opened in 1915 and has a thirty-six-lever frame. It will be abolished when the Cornwall resignalling is completed.

London & North Western Railway

Lichfield City No. 1 is a LNW Type 4 box of 1885, fitted with a fifty-lever frame. On the left, on the balanced bracket, are the Up Main Home 2 signals for the Sutton line and the Walsall line. On the right are the Up Platform Home 2 signals for the Sutton and Walsall lines. The signal box was abolished in October 1992 and the layout considerably simplified.

Lichfield Trent Valley Junction is another LNW Type 4 box. It has a forty-five-lever tumbler frame. The manoeuvre being signalled here is for a train which has terminated at Lichfield City to come forward to make use of the crossover in order that it can run back into the Up platform. This manoeuvre is no longer necessary as the lines at Lichfield City are now signalled bi-directionally. The wooden staircase up to the box has now been replaced by one of steel.

In 1904 the Type 4 was superseded by the Type 5, as seen here at Moreton in the Wirral. Compared to the Type 4, the Type 5 had much deeper windows, overhanging eaves and free bargeboards. The box has had its locking room windows bricked up. It was abolished in 1994.

Altrincham North was another Type 5 box. Notice the unusual angled window designed to give the signalman a better view of the level crossing, which it also controlled. The box was abolished in 1991 and subsequently demolished.

Northampton Bridge Street was opened in 1904 and extended in 1914. It was on the last remaining vestige of the Nene Valley Railway. When this photograph was taken in 1991 the branch was the site of various civil engineers' facilities and industrial sidings, now all gone. The line went out of use in 2005 and the signal box was burnt down. The box had one of the few name boards that dated from the BR era.

Coundon Road station on the Coventry to Nuneaton line opened in 1850 and closed in 1965. The Type 4 signal box opened in 1876. It had a twenty-two-lever frame, latterly reduced to just four. It closed in 2009 and was demolished in 2014.

Wednesbury No. 1 signal box controlled access from the South Staffordshire line to the exchange sidings with the GWR Birmingham–Wolverhampton line. This section of the South Staffordshire line closed in 1993. The box was burnt down shortly after closure.

Canning Street North was at the meeting point of the national network and the Mersey Docks and Harbour Board lines. It also controlled a level crossing. The box, dating from 1900, is another victim of arson. The MDHB lines are all out of use. This photograph was taken in 1990.

Mostyn No. 1 is an unusual LNW Type 4 three-storey box, oversailing on one side. It was opened when the lines here were quadrupled in 1902. It had a forty-lever frame. Mostyn station closed in 1966 and the box was abolished in 2017. The cast-iron footbridge has been demolished. Grade II listed.

In the early days of the railways, signal frames were mostly separate from such shelter as was given to the signalman. The combining of the two came later. In some places a separate frame continued into modern times. One such place was Millbrook station. The original frame dated from 1870 but this was replaced in 1990 by a ten-lever BR frame. In 2004 the signal box closed and control of the line passed to the Marston Vale power box. The frame has been saved for preservation.

LNW/GW Joint

Until 1885 responsibility for the signalling of the LNW/GW joint lines lay with the Joint Lines Engineer's Office in Birkenhead. Their first box design, known as the LNW/GW Joint Type 1, was based on the Saxby & Farmer Type 1 box. This example is at Bromfield on the Shrewsbury–Hereford line. It was opened in 1873 and has a twenty-nine-lever frame. At 145 years old, it is one of the oldest signal boxes still in use.

North Staffordshire Railway

The NSR only ever had two designs of signal box. Foley Crossing is the second of these and was built in 1899. It has a McKenzie & Holland thirty-seven-lever Type 6 frame. The box originally controlled a level crossing, as can be seen from the photograph. It now just controls a pedestrian crossing and is a block post. Notice the curious, and possibly unique, turnstile arrangement for pedestrians. This has since been replaced by a more conventional arrangement.

Mow Cop is another NSR Type 2 box. It was originally fitted with a thirteen-lever McKenzie & Holland frame. This late survivor finally closed in 2002. It was due to be demolished but was saved thanks to the efforts of a local man and has been placed in the village of Mow Cop. The station of Mow Cop and Scholar Green closed in 1964.

Wirral Railway

The Wirral Railway's signal boxes were all built by the Railway Signalling Company, who also supplied the frames. Birkenhead North No. 1 had a forty-lever frame. It was opened in 1888 and abolished in 1994.

Hoylake station signal box was built for the Seacombe, Hoylake & Deeside Railway by the RSC in 1889. It had a twenty-one-lever RSC frame. It was abolished in 1994. The electrically operated intermediate block home signal at Meols was operated from Hoylake box (see signals section).

CLC, MSJ&A and Cambrian

The Cheshire Lines Committee Type 1 signal box is notable in having vertical boarding. Skelton Junction was a Type 1a. Following a fire, the hipped roof was replaced with the structure seen here. The box originally controlled a very busy triple junction, but by the time this photograph was taken only the line to Altrincham had any substantial traffic. In 1991 a DMU passes with a service for Chester.

Navigation Road signal box was built by Saxby & Farmer for the Manchester South Junction & Altrincham Railway in 1882. It was a Type 9 box and had an S&F twenty-one-lever frame, later replaced by a twenty-lever one. On 9 April 1991 a Class 304 EMU heads northwards. The box was abolished later the same year.

Caersws is a Dutton Type 1 box built for the Cambrian Railway in 1891. It retains its original eighteen-lever Dutton frame, although latterly only four levers were in use. The box was abolished in 2011. Grade II listed.

London & South Western Railway

Bere Alston box controlled the junction of the lines to Callington and to Tavistock. Although the latter line is now closed, trains to Gunnislake still have to reverse here. These manoeuvres are no longer controlled from the box but from a ground frame operated by the train crew. The box is an LSW Type 3a and opened in 1890. It closed in September 1970.

Topsham is the only passing place on the single-track line to Exmouth. However, the signal box went out of use in 1988 and the line is controlled from Exmouth Junction. The box is an example of an LSW Type 1, although modified. It dates from *c*.1871 and still has its original twenty-three-lever frame. Grade II listed.

This is Exeter Central signal box. It was originally Exeter 'B', but when the 'A' box was abolished it became simply Exeter Central. It is an LSW Type 4a, opened in 1925 and abolished in February 1970. It was fitted with a thirty-three-lever Tyer frame. The station area is now controlled by Exeter Signalling Centre.

British Railways

Exeter Panel Signal Box was commissioned in 1985. It is equipped with a Westinghouse NX panel. It controls to the west as far as Totnes and Paignton, to the east as far as Cogload Junction, and to Crediton and Exmouth Junctions.

Stafford No. 5 signal box dates from 1952. It is classified as a BR (LMR) Type 14. These were signal boxes designed by the architect's department. No. 5 had a 150-lever frame and controlled the northern approaches to the station. It was abolished along with Stafford No. 4 in 2012. The area is now controlled from the Rugby Rail Operating Centre.

Signals

These are the Up starting signals at Walnut Tree Junction. Centre-pivoted signals like these were used where space or visibility was restricted. The left-hand signal is for the Up Main towards Abercynon and the right-hand one is for the Nantgarw branch, which can be seen curving away to the right. The Nantgarw branch no longer exists, nor do the signals or the signal box, which was abolished in 1998.

Another group of centre-pivoted signals. These are the Up Starters at High Wycombe. They are, left to right: Up Platform line; Up Platform to Up Main (the route that the train has just taken); Up Main. The box on the right is High Wycombe South. Signalling of the line is now controlled by Marylebone Area Signalling Centre, and the trackwork here has been considerably simplified.

Another station controlled from Marylebone ASC is Aylesbury. This is a view south from the platforms taken in 1989. Work on re-signalling is already in hand and soon this collection of semaphores will be no more. The box is Aylesbury South, which closed in 1990 when the re-signalling was completed.

This co-acting signal is at Helsby, at the exit to the Hooton branch. Co-acting signals are used when there is difficulty viewing signals at a distance. The Class 150 is heading for Bangor.

This intermediate block post signal was put in place at Meols following the closure of Meols signal box in 1934. It was worked electrically from Hoylake box. This line is now controlled by the Merseyrail Area Signalling Centre.

Upper quadrant semaphores were often seen on GWR dolls in former GWR areas later coming under LMR control. The finials were often painted white, as here. Cosford signal box can be seen in the distance. It was abolished in 1991 and control transferred to Madeley Junction. The subsidiary signal is for the Down Goods Loop.

At Par we find a GWR signal which has lost its finial and an elevated ground signal. These signals will soon disappear under the Cornwall re-signalling currently underway (2018).

Also due to disappear are these signals at the west end of Truro station. An Azuma train arrives at the station with the 12.04 Penzance to Paddington on 26 September 2018.

The Up Starter at Liskeard. These centre-pivoted signals were made of wood, as were nearly all signals in the early days of signalling, hence the colloquial name of 'boards' for signal arms. On the same gantry is an elevated ground disc.

This triple gantry is for the Up Main Crewe line on the approach to Shrewsbury. The signals are, from left to right: Up Main to Passing Loop; Up Main to Platform 7; Up Main to Platform 4. They are worked by Crewe Junction, the box seen in the background.

This rather unusual signal was at the south end of the Up platform at Yeovil Pen Mill. The signal post is made of concrete at the bottom and wood at the top. It had a route indicator, or 'clack box', as they were colloquially known. The signal was worked by two different levers in the signal box, depending on which route was indicated. In 2008 it was replaced by two upper quadrant signals but was saved and donated to the Yeovil Railway Centre.

This is the well-known 'banjo' signal at Worcester Shrub Hill. It is the Down Main Starter on Platform 3. It effectively divides the platform in two and protects the crossover seen in the background. Below is a calling-on signal, helpfully labelled 'CO'.

A limit of shunt signal at Worcester.

The group of three signals on the bracket are the Down Main Starters at Worcester Shrub Hill. They are, left to right: Down Main to Worcester Foregate Street; Down Main to Shed; and Down Main to Droitwich. Notice the fixed distants. On the right is the only surviving GWR mechanical route indicator or 'clack box' on the network. It controls movements from the Up platform. The 'clack box' displays either H'FORD or B'HAM.

A sight soon to disappear forever. At Croft, the lamp man changes the oil lamp of one of the signals on the Up line. Croft signal box is now closed and the line is controlled from the East Midlands Control Centre.

Tokens are used for single-line working to ensure that no two trains are in the section at the same time. At Buxton the driver of a stone train is surrendering the token for the Hindlow branch.

At some locations token catching apparatus was used. This enabled the driver to drop off the token without having to stop. This set of apparatus was at Lightmoor Junction on the Madeley/Ketley branch.

This is the token for the St Budeaux Victoria Road–Gunnislake branch. Notice the 'key' which enables the train crew to access the ground frame at Bere Alston, where the train has to reverse.

Ground frames were sited in locations remote from signal boxes and were usually worked by the train crew. This is the ground frame for the Wirksworth Incline, which can be seen in the background, which led to a quarry. Wirksworth is now part of the Ecclesbourne Valley Railway.

Signs

A few of these GWR running-in boards have survived here and there on former GWR lines. Kingham is on the Oxford–Worcester line. The name board consists of cast-iron letters screwed on to a wooden base.

There is no doubt that the signs conceived for the newly nationalised British Railways were the best ever on any railway. They were clear and durable – being made of enamelled steel – as well as elegant and colourful. Different colours were allocated to each region: green for the Southern, brown for the Western, maroon for the London Midland, dark blue for the Eastern, pale blue for the Scottish Region, and tangerine for the North Eastern. This sign was seen at Church Stretton.

The advent of Network SouthEast saw almost all the surviving SR green signs replaced. This sign on the signal box at Yeovil Pen Mill was a rare survivor in 1992. It has since been replaced with a black and white sign.

An LMR maroon sign at Colwich Junction.

A pair of signs at Tondu. It is interesting that BR was still producing cast-iron signs as late as 1959.

The railways were compelled by an act of 1845 to erect markers at quarter-mile intervals along their tracks. This was partly to ensure that passengers had been charged the correct fare but more importantly to enable trains, especially when failed, to be located, and for engineering and maintenance purposes. Traditionally distances have always been in miles and chains. Each company had its own style of milepost. This is a GWR example at Roche on the Newquay line and it indicates 290½ miles from Paddington. It is supported on a length of early flat-bottomed rail.

This boundary post is at Verney Junction on the LNW Oxford–Cambridge line.

Victorian elegance, practicality and robustness. This direction sign is on the staircase at Exeter St David's.

Other Buildings and Structures

Bridges and Viaducts

The Cefn Viaduct bridges the River Dee between Ruabon and Chirk. It consists of nineteen arches, each with a span of 60 feet. It is 1,508 feet long and stands 147 feet above the river. The engineer was Henry Robertson. On 28 March 1989 Stanier 4-6-0 No. 5407 crosses the viaduct with a Crewe–Shrewsbury circular special train. Grade II* listed.

The Calstock Viaduct was completed in March 1908. It is constructed of pre-cast concrete blocks. The twelve arches have a span of 60 feet and stand 120 feet above the River Tamar. The viaduct is 1,000 feet long. The engineer was John Charles Long. Grade II* listed.

Also spanning the Tamar is one of the most famous bridges in the world, the Royal Albert Bridge. This amazing structure was conceived by Brunel to finally connect Cornwall to the national network. The main spans are two lenticular wrought-iron trusses, each 455 feet long. They sit 100 feet above the water. The complete bridge including the approaches is 2,187.5 feet long. It was started in 1854 and finished in May 1859. Brunel died later the same year. Grade I listed.

The railway bridge at Worcester Foregate Street was built *c.* 1860 for the West Midland Railway, later part of the GWR. It is constructed of steel, wrought iron and cast iron. The coat of arms in the centre is those of the GWR. The two on either side are coats of arms of the city of Worcester. Grade II listed.

Unlike Continental practice, board crossings did not last very long into the railway age. Instead subways, or more commonly footbridges, were constructed. This very nice example is at Stratford-upon-Avon. Points to note are the pierced, sawtooth valancing, echoing that on the canopy, and the GWR monograms.

Cottages

Level crossings were guarded and operated by level crossing keepers, for whose family accommodation was usually provided. This is the level crossing cottage at Aston by Stone, on the ex-NSR Rugeley–Stone line. Note the Tudor-arched door, the fishscale tiles, the elaborate bargeboards and the diaper brick work.

Another NSR example, this time at Uttoxeter. In this case brick has been used for the window surrounds, and the doorway leading on to the railway has been bricked up.

Accommodation was often provided for railway staff. It was in the railway's interest to have staff on hand and on call. These railway cottages are at Doveholes on the Manchester–Buxton line.

Water

The railway companies had to have the means of supplying the water needed by steam engines, and to that end large tanks were provided, as here at Kemble. The tank is supported on six cast-iron columns, which in turn support cast-iron beams pierced with vertical ovals. Grade II listed.

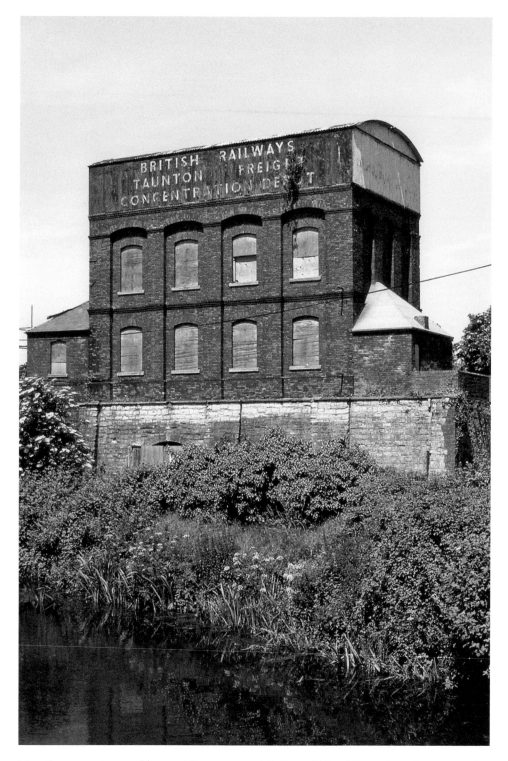

More than meets the eye at Taunton. The water tower is built on old lime kilns and contains two pumping engines which formerly lifted water from the canal. Grade II listed.

And this is where the water ended up. This old water column is at Church Stretton, and apart from the loss of its 'bag' it looks pretty well complete.

Carriage Sheds

Carriages also needed accommodation in order to be maintained and cleaned. However, the advent of the fixed formation train gave rise to the need for a different kind of facility, making traditional carriage sheds redundant. This is the carriage shed at Llandudno Junction. It was demolished in 2000.

The carriage shed at Craven Arms was proposed for demolition by Network Rail in 2003 on grounds of safety. A local group set up the Craven Arms Carriage Sheds Regeneration Association to save the sheds and find an alternative use for them. Unfortunately sufficient funding was not forthcoming and the sheds were demolished in 2004.

Other Buildings

The North Staffordshire Hotel sits opposite Stoke-on-Trent station. It was built in 1848 in a 'Jacobethan' style. Built of brick with ashlar dressings, points to note are the Dutch gables, the mullioned window groups and the diaper brickwork, a particular feature of NSR architecture. The statue is of Josiah Wedgwood. Grade II* listed.

Another building in 'Jacobethan' style is the offices of the Bristol & Exeter Railway at Bristol, designed by S. C .Fripp and completed in 1852. Once again we see the typical features of this style, this time in limestone ashlar: Dutch gables, windows in groups and raised quoins. Grade II*listed.

The South Devon Atmospheric Railway was not one of Brunel's best ideas and the idea of propulsion by the use of a vacuum induced in a tube was soon abandoned. The Starcross Pumping House is a monument to the folly of that idea. It is built of red sandstone in an Italianate style. The chimney, which was originally much taller, is very much like a campanile. It has had a number of uses over the years and is currently used by a fishing and cruising club. Grade I listed.